# Seasonal Cooking Cookbook

## The Ultimate Beginner's Guide To Seasonal Cooking: Fresh, Flavorful Dishes Made Easy

DR JANE T. RYAN

All photographs, and text in this book are original, unless otherwise noted. Any similarity to other photos is purely coincidental.

The information in this book is for educational purposes only and is not intended as a substitute for professional medical advice, diagnosis, or treatment. Always seek the advice of your physician or other qualified health provider with any questions you may have regarding a medical condition.

Limit of Liability/Disclaimer of Warranty: The publisher and author make no representations or warranties with respect to the accuracy or completeness of the contents of this book and specifically disclaim any implied warranties of merchantability or fitness for a particular purpose. The advice and strategies contained herein may not be suitable for every situation. The publisher and author shall not be liable for any loss of profit or any other commercial damages, including but not limited to special, incidental, consequential, or other damages.

Trademarks: All trademarks, service marks, product names, and company names or logos mentioned in this book are the property of their respective owners and are used for identification purposes only. Their use in this book does not imply any affiliation with or endorsement by them

# Welcome to the Art of Seasonal Cooking: A Journey through Nature's Bounty

Welcome, dear culinary enthusiasts, to the captivating world of seasonal cooking, where every dish is a celebration of nature's ever-changing palette! As we embark on this culinary journey, prepare to be enchanted by the vibrant flavors, textures, and aromas that each season graciously bestows upon us.

## Embracing Nature's Rhythms: The Essence of Seasonal Cooking

Seasonal cooking is more than just a culinary trend; it's a philosophy that reconnects us with the rhythms of nature. It invites us to embrace the freshest produce of each season, honoring the natural cycle of growth and harvest. From the tender greens of spring to the hearty root vegetables of winter, each season offers a unique array of ingredients waiting to be transformed into culinary masterpieces.

## Exploring the Bounty of Each Season

In spring, tender shoots of asparagus emerge from the earth, while strawberries blush with sweetness under the warming sun. Summer brings a cornucopia of juicy tomatoes, fragrant herbs, and crisp cucumbers, perfect for refreshing salads and vibrant gazpachos. As the leaves turn golden and the air grows crisper, autumn invites us to savor the earthy flavors of squash, apples, and pears, crafting comforting soups and hearty stews. And when winter blankets the land in snow, we turn to hearty root vegetables, robust greens, and citrus fruits to brighten our plates and warm our souls.

## The Art of Seasonal Pairings: Harmonizing Flavors and Textures

One of the joys of seasonal cooking lies in the art of pairing ingredients to create harmonious flavors and textures. From the delicate balance of sweet and savory in a summer peach salad to the comforting embrace of roasted root vegetables with fragrant herbs, each dish tells a story of the season it represents. Whether you're experimenting with bold spices or celebrating the simplicity of fresh, local ingredients, seasonal cooking offers endless opportunities for culinary creativity.

### Celebrating Tradition and Innovation

While seasonal cooking honors age-old traditions passed down through generations, it also invites us to explore new techniques, flavors, and cultural influences. From traditional harvest festivals to innovative farm-to-table dining experiences, the world of seasonal cooking is as diverse and dynamic as the landscapes that inspire it.

### Join Us on a Culinary Adventure

So, dear friends, as we embark on this culinary adventure together, let us revel in the beauty of nature's bounty, celebrate the richness of each season, and savor the magic of seasonal cooking. From farm-fresh markets to cozy kitchen gatherings, let us gather around the table and share in the joy of good food, good company, and the timeless rhythms of the seasons. Welcome to the art of seasonal cooking—where every meal is a celebration of nature's abundance and a feast for the senses. Let's savor every moment together!

# Introduction

# Unlocking the Power of Seasonal Eating

Welcome to the delightful world of seasonal eating, where fresh, locally sourced ingredients take center stage in creating wholesome, flavorful dishes. In this seasonal cooking cookbook, we embark on a journey to discover the myriad benefits of embracing the natural rhythms of the seasons and celebrating the abundance of each harvest.

### Nutritional Superiority: Harnessing the Power of Freshness

Seasonal eating is not only a feast for the senses but also a boon for our health. By consuming fruits, vegetables, and herbs at the peak of their ripeness, we ensure maximum nutritional value in every bite. From vitamin-rich berries in summer to vitamin C-packed citrus fruits in winter, seasonal eating provides a diverse array of nutrients essential for optimal health and vitality.

### Environmental Sustainability: Nurturing the Earth

Embracing seasonal eating is an act of environmental stewardship. By supporting local farmers and choosing ingredients that are in season, we reduce the carbon footprint associated with long-distance transportation and minimize the use of harmful pesticides and chemicals. Seasonal eating fosters a deeper connection to the land and promotes sustainable farming practices that preserve natural ecosystems for generations to come.

## Economic Support: Investing in Local Communities

When we prioritize seasonal ingredients, we not only support local farmers and producers but also contribute to the vitality of our communities. By purchasing from farmers' markets, community-supported agriculture (CSA) programs, and independent grocers, we help sustain local economies and promote food sovereignty. Seasonal eating fosters a sense of community and strengthens the bonds between producers and consumers, creating a more resilient and equitable food system.

## Culinary Creativity: Embracing the Flavors of Each Season

Seasonal eating inspires culinary creativity and encourages us to explore new flavors, textures, and cooking techniques. From delicate spring salads to hearty winter stews, each season offers a rich tapestry of ingredients waiting to be transformed into delicious meals. By embracing the flavors of the season, we embark on a culinary adventure that celebrates the diversity of local produce and honors the traditions of regional cuisine.

## Emotional Well-Being: Nourishing Body and Soul

Beyond nourishing our bodies, seasonal eating nourishes our souls. There is a profound sense of satisfaction that comes from eating food that is fresh, flavorful, and thoughtfully prepared. By savoring the tastes and textures of each season, we cultivate mindfulness and gratitude for the abundance that surrounds us. Seasonal eating invites us to slow down, savor the moment, and appreciate the simple pleasures of a well-cooked meal shared with loved ones.

## Embracing the Seasons, One Bite at a Time

In this seasonal cooking cookbook, we invite you to embark on a journey of discovery and delight as we explore the benefits of seasonal eating. From vibrant salads to hearty soups, from summer grilling to winter roasts, let us celebrate the beauty of each season and savor the flavors of nature's bounty. Together, let us embrace the joys of seasonal eating and cultivate a deeper connection to the food we eat, the land that sustains us, and the communities we call home.

Bon appétit!

# Exploring the Culinary Seasons A Guide to Using This Seasonal Cooking Cookbook

Welcome to the vibrant world of seasonal cooking, where each turn of the calendar brings new flavors, textures, and culinary possibilities. This cookbook is your passport to exploring the bounty of each season and harnessing the power of fresh, locally sourced ingredients. Here's how to make the most of your culinary journey through the seasons:

### Seasonal Navigation: Understanding the Rhythms of Nature

Before diving into recipes, take a moment to familiarize yourself with the seasonal calendar and the ingredients that shine during each time of the year. Whether it's the crisp greens of spring, the sun-ripened fruits of summer, the hearty vegetables of autumn, or the comforting staples of winter, understanding the seasonal landscape will guide your culinary adventures.

### Ingredient Spotlight: Celebrating Seasonal Staples

Each season boasts its own cast of culinary stars, from delicate herbs and tender greens to robust root vegetables and succulent fruits. In this cookbook, you'll find detailed profiles of seasonal ingredients, highlighting their flavor profiles, nutritional benefits, and culinary versatility. Use these profiles as a guide to selecting the freshest, most flavorful ingredients for your recipes.

### Recipe Selection: From Farm to Table

Our cookbook features a diverse array of recipes designed to showcase the best of each season's bounty. From simple salads and soups to hearty mains and decadent desserts, there's something for every palate and occasion. As you browse through the recipes, consider the ingredients you have on hand, the flavors you're craving, and the culinary adventures you're ready to embark upon.

### Seasonal Substitutions: Embracing Flexibility in the Kitchen

Don't be afraid to get creative and make substitutions based on what's available and in season. If a recipe calls for strawberries but you have raspberries on hand, feel free to make the swap. Similarly, if a recipe features a seasonal ingredient that's not readily available in your area, consider alternatives that capture the spirit of the season.

## Culinary Exploration: Making It Your Own

While our recipes serve as a starting point, don't hesitate to add your own personal touch and culinary flair. Experiment with different herbs, spices, and cooking techniques to tailor recipes to your taste preferences and dietary needs. The kitchen is your culinary playground, and seasonal cooking offers endless opportunities for creativity and exploration.

## Sharing the Joy: Inviting Others to the Table

Food has a wonderful power to unite people and generate enduring memories. Whether you're cooking for family, friends, or yourself, embrace the joy of sharing delicious meals made with love and care. Invite others to join you in the kitchen, swap stories and recipes, and savor the simple pleasures of good food and good company.

## A Seasonal Feast for the Senses

As you embark on your culinary journey through the seasons, remember that seasonal cooking is as much about nourishing the body as it is about feeding the soul. Embrace the rhythms of nature, celebrate the diversity of flavors, and savor each moment spent in the kitchen. With this cookbook as your guide, may your meals be a celebration of the seasons, a tribute to the earth, and a testament to the joy of seasonal cooking.

Bon appétit!

# CHAPTER 1

# SPRING DELIGHTS

# Fresh Spring Greens Salad

Ingredients:

- Mixed spring greens (such as spinach, arugula, and kale)
- Cherry tomatoes, halved
- Cucumber, thinly sliced
- Red onion, thinly sliced
- Avocado, diced
- Roasted seeds or nuts, including pumpkin seeds, walnuts, or almonds
- Crumbled feta cheese or goat cheese (optional)

Dressing:

- Extra virgin olive oil
- Balsamic vinegar
- Dijon mustard
- Honey (or, for a vegan alternative, maple syrup)
- Salt and pepper to taste

Time of Preparation:

- Preparation time: 15 minutes
- Total time: 15 minutes

Procedures:

- Wash and dry the mixed spring greens thoroughly. Any big leaves should be torn into bite-sized pieces and added to a large salad bowl.

- Add the cherry tomatoes, cucumber slices, thinly sliced red onion, diced avocado, and toasted nuts or seeds to the bowl.
- To create the dressing, combine the extra virgin olive oil, honey (or maple syrup), balsamic vinegar, Dijon mustard, salt, and pepper in a small container or bowl.
- Drizzle the dressing over the salad ingredients in the bowl.
- Toss the salad gently until the dressing is evenly distributed.
- If desired, sprinkle crumbled feta cheese or goat cheese over the top of the salad.

Tips and Tricks:

- Use a mix of tender and crunchy greens for a variety of textures in your salad.
- Toasting nuts or seeds before adding them to the salad enhances their flavor and crunch.
- Adjust the ratio of oil to vinegar in the dressing according to your taste preferences.

Nutritional Value Per Serving:

- Calories: 150-200 kcal
- Fat: 10-15g
- Carbohydrates: 10-15g
- Protein: 5-8g
- Fiber: 3-5g

Health Benefits:

- Rich in vitamins and minerals, including vitamin A, vitamin C, vitamin K, folate, and potassium.
- Rich in fibre, which supports healthy digestion and gives you a feeling of fullness and satisfaction.
- The antioxidants in the vegetables and olive oil help reduce inflammation and protect against chronic diseases.

Packaging and Storing:

- To keep the salad fresh for two or three days, refrigerate it in an airtight container.
- If making the salad ahead of time, store the dressing separately and toss it with the salad just before serving to prevent wilting.

## Precautions and Post-Caution:

- Wash all vegetables thoroughly before using them in the salad to remove any dirt or contaminants.
- Be cautious when cutting ingredients, especially when using sharp knives.
- Always use fresh, high-quality ingredients to ensure the best flavor and nutritional value.

## Safety Caution:

- Avoid leaving the salad at room temperature for extended periods, especially in warm weather, to prevent bacterial growth.
- If you have food allergies or dietary restrictions, be mindful of the ingredients you use and make substitutions as necessary.
- Enjoy your refreshing and nutritious Fresh Spring Greens Salad!

# Asparagus and Lemon Risotto

Ingredients:

- One bunch of asparagus, thinly sliced into small pieces.
- 1 onion, finely chopped
- 2 cloves of garlic, minced
- 1 ½ cups Arborio rice
- Four cups heated vegetable or chicken broth
- ½ cup dry white wine (optional)
- Zest and juice of 1 lemon
- ½ cup grated Parmesan cheese
- Salt and pepper to taste
- Fresh parsley, chopped (for garnish)
- Olive oil

Time of Preparation:

- Preparation time: 10 minutes
- Cooking time: 30 minutes
- Total time: 40 minutes

Procedures:

- In a large skillet or pot, heat a drizzle of olive oil over medium heat. Add the chopped onion and cook for 3–4 minutes, or until transparent.
- Cook the minced garlic in the skillet for a further one to two minutes, or until it becomes fragrant.
- Add the Arborio rice and heat for one to two minutes, stirring frequently, until the rice is lightly browned.
- If using, add the white wine and toss often while cooking until the rice absorbs it.
- Begin adding the warm broth to the rice, one ladleful at a time, stirring frequently and allowing each addition to be absorbed before adding more.
- After about 15 minutes of cooking, add the asparagus pieces to the risotto and continue adding broth and stirring until the rice is creamy and tender, and the asparagus is cooked but still slightly crisp, about 5-7 minutes more.
- Garnish the risotto with chopped fresh parsley before serving.

Tips and Tricks:

- Use homemade broth or low-sodium broth for better control over the salt content of your risotto.
- Stir the risotto constantly to encourage the release of starch from the rice, resulting in a creamy texture.
- Add the asparagus towards the end of cooking to maintain its vibrant color and crisp texture.

Nutritional Value Per Serving:

- Calories: 300-350 kcal
- Fat: 7-10g
- Carbohydrates: 50-60g
- Protein: 10-15g
- Fiber: 3-5g

Health Benefits:

- Asparagus is a good source of fiber, vitamins A, C, E, and K, as well as folate and chromium.
- Arborio rice provides complex carbohydrates for sustained energy and is low in fat and cholesterol.
- Lemon adds a refreshing flavor and is rich in vitamin C, antioxidants, and citric acid, which aids digestion.

Packaging and Storing:

- Risotto is best served immediately after cooking to maintain its creamy texture.
- Leftover risotto can be stored in an airtight container in the refrigerator for up to 2 days.
- Reheat the risotto gently on the stovetop with a splash of broth or water to restore its creamy consistency.

Precautions and Post-Caution:

- Be cautious when adding hot broth to the risotto to avoid splashing and burns.
- Ensure the asparagus is thoroughly washed and trimmed before adding it to the risotto.
- Refrigerate leftover risotto promptly to prevent bacterial growth.

Safety Caution:

- Use caution when handling knives and hot surfaces during the preparation and cooking process.
- Always use fresh ingredients and store perishable items properly to avoid foodborne illness.
- Enjoy your flavorful and creamy Asparagus and Lemon Risotto!

# Strawberry Rhubarb Crisp

Ingredients:

- 4 cups sliced rhubarb
- 4 cups sliced strawberries
- 1 cup granulated sugar
- 2 tablespoons cornstarch
- 1 teaspoon vanilla extract
- 1 cup all-purpose flour
- 1 cup old-fashioned rolled oats
- 1 cup brown sugar
- 1/2 cup cold unsalted butter, diced
- 1/2 teaspoon ground cinnamon
- Pinch of salt

Time of Preparation:

- Preparation time: 15 minutes
- Baking time: 45-50 minutes
- Total time: 60-65 minutes

Procedures:

- Preheat your oven to 350°F (175°C). Grease a 9x13-inch baking dish.
- In a large bowl, combine the sliced rhubarb and strawberries.
- In a separate small bowl, mix the granulated sugar and cornstarch. After sprinkling the mixture over the fruit, gently toss to incorporate.
- Toss the fruit combination once more to ensure that the vanilla extract is distributed evenly.
- Spread the fruit mixture equally in the baking dish that has been prepared.

Crisp Topping:

- In a medium bowl, combine the flour, oats, brown sugar, diced cold butter, ground cinnamon, and salt.
- Work the butter into the dry ingredients with your fingertips or a pastry cutter until the mixture resembles coarse crumbs.
- Sprinkle the crisp topping evenly over the fruit in the baking dish.

Baking:

- Place the baking dish in the preheated oven and bake for 45-50 minutes, or until the fruit is bubbling and the topping is golden brown.
- Before serving, take the crisp out of the oven and let it to cool for a few minutes..

Tips and Tricks:

- Use fresh rhubarb and strawberries for the best flavor and texture.
- Adjust the amount of sugar according to the sweetness of your strawberries and personal preference.
- For added texture and flavor, you can mix chopped nuts (such as almonds or pecans) into the crisp topping.

Nutritional Value Per Serving:

- Calories: 250-300 kcal
- Fat: 10-15g
- Carbohydrates: 40-50g
- Protein: 2-4g
- Fiber: 3-5g

### Health Benefits:

- Vitamin C, potassium, calcium, and vitamin K are all present in good amounts in rhubarb.
- Strawberries are rich in antioxidants, vitamin C, manganese, and fiber, which contribute to heart health and may help regulate blood sugar levels.

### Packaging and Storing:

- Allow the crisp to cool completely before storing leftovers in an airtight container in the refrigerator.
- Reheat individual servings in the microwave or oven before serving.

### Precautions and Post-Caution:

- Be cautious when handling rhubarb, as its leaves contain oxalic acid, which can be toxic if ingested.
- Ensure that all rhubarb leaves are removed and discarded before using the stalks in the recipe.
- Let the crisp cool adequately before serving to avoid burns from the hot fruit filling.

### Safety Caution:

- Use caution when working with sharp knives and hot ovens.
- Store leftovers properly to prevent foodborne illness, and discard any leftovers that have been sitting at room temperature for more than two hours.
- Enjoy your delicious and comforting Strawberry Rhubarb Crisp!

# Lemon Asparagus Pasta

Ingredients:

- 8 ounces (225 grammes) of pasta, like fettuccine or spaghetti
- One bunch of asparagus, thinly sliced into small pieces.
- Two tsp olive oil
- three minced garlic cloves, one lemon's zest, and juice
- Grated Parmesan cheese, 1/4 cup (plus more for serving)
- Salt and pepper to taste
- Fresh parsley, chopped (for garnish)

Time of Preparation:

- Preparation time: 10 minutes
- Cooking time: 15 minutes
- Total time: 25 minutes

Procedures:

- Pasta should be cooked as directed on the package until it is al dente. With the exception of roughly 1/2 cup of pasta water, drain and set aside.

- In a large skillet over medium heat, warm the olive oil while the pasta cooks. Add the minced garlic and simmer for one to two minutes, or until fragrant.
- Add the asparagus pieces to the skillet and cook, stirring occasionally, until they are bright green and slightly tender, about 5-7 minutes.
- Add the cooked pasta to the skillet with the asparagus. Toss to combine.
- Add the lemon zest and lemon juice to the skillet, tossing to coat the pasta and asparagus evenly.
- Add a small amount of the pasta water that was set aside at a time to the pasta if it seems dry, stirring until the appropriate consistency is achieved.
- Add the grated Parmesan cheese and taste and adjust the seasoning.
- Garnish with chopped fresh parsley and additional grated Parmesan cheese before serving.

Tips and Tricks:

- Cook the asparagus just until it is tender-crisp to retain its vibrant color and nutrients.
- Reserve some pasta water to help create a silky sauce that coats the pasta evenly.
- For optimal taste and texture, use freshly grated Parmesan cheese.

Nutritional Value Per Serving:

- Calories: 300-350 kcal
- Fat: 10-15g
- Carbohydrates: 40-50g
- Protein: 10-15g
- Fiber: 5-8g

Health Benefits:

- Along with fibre, folate, vitamins A, C, E, and K, and chromium, a trace mineral that aids in blood sugar regulation, asparagus is a wonderful source of these nutrients.
- Lemon adds a burst of citrus flavor and is rich in vitamin C, antioxidants, and citric acid, which aids digestion and may improve skin health.
- Packaging and Storing:
- Any leftovers can be kept in the fridge for up to two days if they are kept in an airtight container.

- Reheat individual servings in the microwave or on the stovetop with a splash of water or broth to prevent drying out.

Precautions and Post-Caution:

- Be cautious not to overcook the asparagus, as it can become mushy and lose its flavor and nutrients.
- Ensure the garlic does not burn while cooking; adjust the heat as needed.
- Avoid reheating the pasta multiple times to prevent it from becoming mushy.

Safety Caution:

- Use caution when handling hot pasta and pans.
- Wash the asparagus thoroughly and trim off any tough ends before cooking.
- To stop bacteria from growing, store leftovers in the refrigerator as soon as possible.
- Enjoy your light and flavorful Lemon Asparagus Pasta!

# Chapter 2

# Summer Sizzlers

# Grilled Vegetable Medley

Ingredients:

- 2 medium zucchinis, sliced
- 1 large red bell pepper, sliced
- 1 large yellow bell pepper, sliced
- 1 medium eggplant, sliced
- 1 red onion, sliced
- 2 tablespoons olive oil
- 2 cloves garlic, minced
- Salt and pepper to taste
- 1 teaspoon dried Italian herbs (optional)
- Balsamic glaze for drizzling (optional)
- Fresh herbs for garnish (optional)

Time of preparation:

- Preparation Time: 20 minutes
- Cooking Time: 15 minutes
- Total Time: 35 minutes
- Servings: 4

Procedure:

- Prepare the Grill:
- Adjust the heat on your grill to medium-high (375–400°F/190–200°C).

Prepare the Vegetables:

- Wash and slice the zucchinis, red bell pepper, yellow bell pepper, eggplant, and red onion into even slices.

Marinate the Vegetables:

- In a large bowl, combine the sliced vegetables with olive oil, minced garlic, salt, pepper, and dried Italian herbs if using. Toss well to coat evenly.

Grill the Vegetables:

- Transfer the marinated vegetables to the grill and warm it.
- Grill until they are tender and have grill marks, about 5 to 7 minutes per side.
- Remove the grilled vegetables from the grill and arrange them on a serving platter.
- Drizzle with balsamic glaze if desired and garnish with fresh herbs.

Tips and Tricks:

- Ensure that the vegetables are sliced evenly to ensure even cooking.
- You can use a grill basket or grill pan to prevent smaller pieces from falling through the grill grates.
- Don't overcrowd the grill to allow the vegetables to cook evenly and get those nice grill marks.

Nutritional Value per Serving (approximate):

- Calories: 120 kcal
- Carbohydrates: 12g
- Fat: 7g
- Protein: 3g
- Fiber: 4g
- Vitamin A: 35% DV
- Vitamin C: 160% DV
- Potassium: 15% DV

Health Benefits:

- Rich in vitamins, minerals, and antioxidants.
- Low in calories and high in fiber, making it great for weight management.
- Helps to promote healthy digestion and supports overall gut health.
- Provides essential nutrients for maintaining healthy skin, hair, and nails.

Packaging and Storing:

- Store leftover grilled vegetable medley in an airtight container in the refrigerator for up to 3 days.
- Before serving, reheat in the oven or microwave until well heated.

Precautions and Post-Caution:

- Always handle hot grill surfaces with caution to avoid burns.
- Make sure the grill is properly cleaned and maintained to prevent food contamination.
- Wash vegetables thoroughly before slicing and grilling to remove any dirt or debris.

Safety Caution:

- Use long-handled tongs and spatulas when handling food on the grill to avoid burns.
- Keep children and pets away from the grill area to prevent accidents.
- Enjoy your delicious and nutritious Grilled Vegetable Medley!

# Watermelon Feta Salad

Ingredients:

- 4 cups cubed watermelon
- 1 cup crumbled feta cheese
- 1/4 cup fresh mint leaves, chopped
- 2 tablespoons extra virgin olive oil
- 1 tablespoon balsamic vinegar
- Salt and pepper to taste

Optional:

- 1/4 cup sliced red onion or 1/4 cup sliced cucumber for added flavor and texture

Time of preparation:

- Preparation Time: 15 minutes
- Total Time: 15 minutes
- Servings: 4

Procedure:

Prepare the Ingredients:

- Clean the watermelon and chop it into little chunks.
- Crumble the feta cheese.

- Chop the fresh mint leaves.

Assemble the Salad:

- In a large mixing bowl, combine the cubed watermelon, crumbled feta cheese, and chopped mint leaves.
- If using, add sliced red onion or cucumber for extra flavor and texture.

Dress the Salad:

- Over the salad, drizzle some extra virgin olive oil and balsamic vinegar.
- To taste, add salt and pepper for seasoning.
- Till every component of the salad is equally covered with dressing, gently toss it.

Serve:

- Transfer the watermelon feta salad to a serving dish or individual plates.
- Garnish with additional mint leaves if desired.

Tips and Tricks:

- For optimal flavour, use a watermelon that is both ripe and sweet.
- For a refreshing twist, chill the watermelon in the refrigerator before assembling the salad.
- Use high-quality feta cheese for optimal creaminess and flavor.
- Adjust the amount of mint leaves and balsamic vinegar according to your taste preferences.

Nutritional Value per Serving (approximate):

- Calories: 180 kcal
- Carbohydrates: 14g
- Fat: 12g
- Protein: 6g
- Fiber: 1g
- Vitamin A: 20% DV
- Vitamin C: 25% DV
- Calcium: 20% DV

Health Benefits:

- Watermelon is rich in hydration, vitamins A and C, and antioxidants, promoting healthy skin and immune function.
- Feta cheese provides protein and calcium for bone health.
- Mint leaves aid digestion and add a refreshing flavor to the salad.
- Olive oil contributes heart-healthy monounsaturated fats and antioxidants.

Packaging and Storing:

- Watermelon feta salad is best served fresh but can be stored in an airtight container in the refrigerator for up to 2 days.
- Keep the salad chilled to maintain its freshness and prevent the watermelon from becoming mushy.

Precautions and Post-Caution:

- Handle the knife and cutting board carefully when cutting the watermelon to avoid accidents.
- To stop bacteria from growing, store leftovers in the refrigerator as soon as possible.

Safety Caution:

- To avoid contamination, wash your hands well before handling food.
- Cut the items into small pieces using a clean knife and chopping board.
- Perishable materials should be kept chilled until needed.
- Enjoy the refreshing and flavorful Watermelon Feta Salad!

# BBQ Chicken Skewers with Mango Salsa

Ingredients:

For BBQ Chicken Skewers:

- One pound (450 grammes) of skinless, boneless chicken breasts, diced into 1-inch pieces
- 1/4 cup BBQ sauce
- 2 tablespoons olive oil
- 1 teaspoon smoked paprika
- 1 teaspoon garlic powder
- Salt and pepper to taste
- Wooden or metal skewers
- For Mango Salsa:
- 1 ripe mango, diced
- 1/4 cup red onion, finely chopped
- 1/4 cup fresh cilantro, chopped
- 1 jalapeño pepper, seeded and minced
- Juice of 1 lime
- Salt to taste

Time of preparation:

- Preparation Time: 20 minutes
- Marinating Time: 30 minutes
- Cooking Time: 15 minutes

- Total Time: 1 hour 5 minutes
- Servings: 4

Procedure:

Marinate the Chicken:

- In a bowl, combine the cubed chicken with BBQ sauce, olive oil, smoked paprika, garlic powder, salt, and pepper. Toss until the chicken is evenly coated For at least half an hour, marinate covered in the fridge.Prepare the Mango Salsa:
- In another bowl, combine the diced mango, chopped red onion, cilantro, minced jalapeño pepper, lime juice, and salt. Mix well to combine. Adjust seasoning to taste. Keep chilled and covered until you're ready to serve.

Assemble the Skewers:

- Preheat the grill to medium-high heat.
- Thread the marinated chicken pieces onto skewers, leaving a little space between each piece.

Grill the Chicken Skewers:

- Place the skewers on the preheated grill and cook for about 6-8 minutes per side or until the chicken is cooked through and has grill marks.

Serve:

- Transfer the grilled chicken skewers to a serving platter.
- Serve with the mango salsa on the side or spooned over the top of the skewers.

Tips and Tricks:

- Soak wooden skewers in water for at least 30 minutes before threading to prevent them from burning on the grill.
- Cut the chicken into uniform-sized pieces to ensure even cooking.
- Baste the chicken with extra BBQ sauce while grilling for added flavor and moisture.
- Use ripe mangoes for the salsa for the best flavor and texture.

Nutritional Value per Serving (approximate):

- Calories: 280 kcal

- Carbohydrates: 20g
- Fat: 9g
- Protein: 25g
- Fiber: 3g
- Vitamin A: 25% DV
- Vitamin C: 60% DV
- Iron: 6% DV

Health Benefits:

- Chicken is a lean source of protein, essential for muscle growth and repair.
- Mangoes are rich in vitamins A and C, antioxidants, and fiber, promoting immune function and digestive health.
- Jalapeño peppers contain capsaicin, which may help boost metabolism and reduce inflammation.

Packaging and Storing:

- Store any leftover chicken skewers and mango salsa separately in airtight containers in the refrigerator for up to 2 days.
- Reheat the chicken skewers in the microwave or oven until warmed through before serving.

Precautions and Post-Caution:

- Ensure chicken is cooked to an internal temperature of 165°F (75°C) to prevent foodborne illness.
- Use separate cutting boards and utensils for raw chicken and other ingredients to avoid cross-contamination.
- Refrigerate leftovers promptly to prevent bacterial growth.

Safety Caution:

- Handle raw chicken with care to avoid spreading bacteria.
- Keep hands, utensils, and surfaces clean during food preparation.
- Use a meat thermometer to check the internal temperature of the chicken for doneness.

- Enjoy the delicious BBQ Chicken Skewers with Mango Salsa for a flavorful and satisfying meal!

## BBQ Shrimp Skewers

Ingredients:

- 1 lb (450g) large shrimp, peeled and deveined
- 1/4 cup BBQ sauce
- 2 tablespoons olive oil
- 2 cloves garlic, minced
- 1 teaspoon smoked paprika
- 1/2 teaspoon cayenne pepper (optional for added heat)
- Salt and pepper to taste
- Wooden or metal skewers

Time of preparation:

- Preparation Time: 15 minutes
- Marinating Time: 30 minutes

- Cooking Time: 8-10 minutes
- Total Time: 55 minutes
- Servings: 4

Procedure:

Marinate the Shrimp:

- In a bowl, combine the peeled and deveined shrimp with BBQ sauce, olive oil, minced garlic, smoked paprika, cayenne pepper (if using), salt, and pepper. Toss until the shrimp are evenly coated. Cover and Allow the flavours to mingle for at least half an hour by covering and refrigerating.

Get the skewers ready:

- To keep wooden skewers from burning on the grill, soak them in water for at least half an hour.
- As you thread the marinated prawns onto the skewers, make sure to leave a small gap between them.

Preheat the Grill:

- Preheat your grill to medium-high heat.

Grill the Shrimp Skewers:

- Place the shrimp skewers on the preheated grill.
- Grill for 2-3 minutes per side, or until the shrimp are pink and opaque, and have grill marks.

Serve:

- Place the prawn skewers that have been grilled onto a serving plate.
- If desired, garnish with freshly cut cilantro or parsley.

Tips and Tricks:

- Use fresh or frozen shrimp that has been thawed for this recipe.
- Don't over-marinate the shrimp as the acidity in the BBQ sauce can break down the shrimp.
- If using wooden skewers, thread the shrimp onto two skewers instead of one to prevent them from spinning when flipping on the grill.
- To keep the grill grates from sticking, oil them before cooking.

Nutritional Value per Serving (approximate):

- Calories: 160 kcal
- Carbohydrates: 5g
- Fat: 7g
- Protein: 20g
- Fiber: 0g
- Vitamin A: 15% DV
- Vitamin C: 6% DV
- Iron: 10% DV

Health Benefits:

- Shrimp is low in calories and high in protein, making it a nutritious seafood choice.
- Omega-3 fatty acids, which are advantageous for heart health, are abundant in prawns.
- Garlic and paprika provide antioxidants and anti-inflammatory properties.
- BBQ sauce, when used in moderation, adds flavor without adding significant calories.

Packaging and Storing:

- Any leftover BBQ prawn skewers can be kept in the fridge for up to two days in an airtight container.
- Reheat the shrimp in a skillet or microwave until warmed through before serving.

Precautions and Post-Caution:

- Ensure that shrimp are cooked to an internal temperature of 145°F (63°C) to prevent foodborne illness.
- Avoid overcooking shrimp as they can become rubbery and lose their flavor.
- Discard any leftover marinade that has come into contact with raw shrimp to prevent contamination.

Safety Caution:

- Keep raw shrimp and cooked shrimp separate to avoid cross-contamination.
- Wash hands, utensils, and surfaces thoroughly after handling raw shrimp.
- Use a food thermometer to check the internal temperature of the shrimp for doneness.
- Enjoy the delicious BBQ Shrimp Skewers as a flavorful appetizer or main dish!

# Chapter 3

# Autumn Harvest

# Apple Pecan Stuffed Acorn Squash

Ingredients:

- 2 medium acorn squash
- 2 tablespoons olive oil
- Salt and pepper to taste
- 1 cup chopped pecans
- 2 medium apples, diced (such as Granny Smith or Honeycrisp)
- 1 small onion, diced
- 2 cloves garlic, minced
- 1 teaspoon ground cinnamon
- 1/2 teaspoon ground nutmeg
- 1/4 cup maple syrup
- 1/2 cup dried cranberries
- 1/2 cup breadcrumbs (optional)
- Fresh parsley for garnish (optional)

Time of preparation:

- Preparation Time: 15 minutes
- Cooking Time: 45 minutes
- Total Time: 1 hour

Procedure:

- Preheat your oven to 375°F (190°C).
- Scoop out the seeds and fibres from the acorn squash by cutting it in half lengthwise.
- After applying a thin layer of olive oil, season the insides of the squash halves with salt and pepper. Put them, face down, on a parchment paper-lined baking sheet.
- When a fork pierces the squash, it should be soft after 30 to 35 minutes of baking in a preheated oven.
- Heat the remaining olive oil in a skillet over medium heat while the squash bakes.
- Add the chopped pecans and toast them for 2-3 minutes until fragrant.
- Stir in the diced apples, onion, and garlic, and cook until softened, about 5-7 minutes.
- Add the ground cinnamon, ground nutmeg, maple syrup, and dried cranberries to the skillet, stirring to combine.
- Cook for an additional 2-3 minutes until the mixture is heated through and well combined.
- If desired, add breadcrumbs to the mixture to help bind the stuffing together.
- Once the squash halves are tender, remove them from the oven and carefully flip them over.
- Fill each squash half with the apple-pecan stuffing mixture, dividing evenly among the halves.
- Return the stuffed squash to the oven and bake for an additional 10-15 minutes until heated through and golden brown on top.

Nutritional Value per Serving:

- Calories: 320
- Total Fat: 18g
- Saturated Fat: 2g
- Cholesterol: 0mg
- Sodium: 20mg
- Total Carbohydrate: 40g
- Dietary Fiber: 6g
- Sugars: 20g
- Protein: 4g

Health Benefits:

- Rich in fiber, vitamins, and minerals.
- Pecans provide heart-healthy fats and protein.
- Apples offer antioxidants and dietary fiber.
- Acorn squash is a good source of vitamin C, potassium, and antioxidants.

Packaging and Storing:

- Leftover stuffed squash can be kept in the fridge for up to three to four days if stored in an airtight container.
- To reheat, microwave individual servings or warm them in the oven at 350°F (175°C) until heated through.

Precautions and Safety:

- Use caution when handling hot squash and stuffing.
- Ensure the squash is cooked thoroughly before consuming.
- Check for any allergies to nuts or other ingredients among your guests before serving.

Post-Caution:

- Refrigerate leftovers promptly to avoid spoilage.
- Reheat leftovers to an internal temperature of 165°F (74°C) before consuming.

# Butternut Squash Soup

Ingredients:

- 1 large butternut squash, peeled, seeded, and diced
- 1 onion, diced
- 2 cloves garlic, minced
- 2 carrots, peeled and diced
- 2 stalks celery, diced
- 4 cups vegetable broth
- 1 teaspoon dried thyme
- 1/2 teaspoon ground nutmeg
- Salt and pepper to taste
- 2 tablespoons olive oil

Optional toppings:

- roasted pumpkin seeds, drizzle of cream, chopped fresh herbs

Time of preparation:

- Preparation Time: 15 minutes
- Cooking Time: 30 minutes
- Total Time: 45 minutes

Procedure:

- Warm up the olive oil in a big pot over medium heat.
- Add diced onion, garlic, carrots, and celery. Sauté until onions are translucent and vegetables are tender, about 5-7 minutes.
- Add ground nutmeg and dried thyme to the pot with the cubed butternut squash. Stir to combine.
- Pour in vegetable broth, ensuring that the vegetables are covered. Bring to a boil, then reduce heat to low and simmer for 20-25 minutes, or until the squash is fork-tender.
- Once the squash and vegetables are cooked, remove the pot from the heat.
- Puree the soup with an immersion blender until it's creamy and smooth. Alternatively, pour the soup into a blender in batches and process until smooth. When combining hot liquids, exercise caution.
- Add salt and pepper to taste, and adjust the seasoning if necessary.
- If the soup is too thick, you can thin it out with additional vegetable broth or water until you reach your desired consistency.
- Serve hot, garnished with optional toppings like roasted pumpkin seeds, a drizzle of cream, or chopped fresh herbs.

Nutritional Value per Serving:

- Calories: 150
- Total Fat: 5g
- Saturated Fat: 1g
- Cholesterol: 0mg
- Sodium: 650mg
- Total Carbohydrate: 26g
- Dietary Fiber: 6g
- Sugars: 8g
- Protein: 3g

Health Benefits:

- Butternut squash is rich in vitamins A and C, potassium, and fiber.
- It's a good choice for managing weight because it's low in calories and fat.
- Before storing the soup in sealed jars, let it cool fully.

- Keep refrigerated for a maximum of four to five days.
- Freeze the soup for up to three months in freezer-safe containers for extended storage..

Precautions and Safety:

- Be careful when handling hot soup and using the blender to avoid burns.
- Use caution when pureeing hot liquids to prevent splattering.

Post-Caution:

- When reheating the soup, ensure it reaches a safe internal temperature of 165°F (74°C) to prevent foodborne illness.
- Discard any leftover soup that has been left at room temperature for more than 2 hours to avoid bacterial contamination.

# Pumpkin Spice Muffins

Ingredients:

- 2 cups all-purpose flour
- 1 teaspoon baking powder
- 1/2 teaspoon baking soda
- 1/2 teaspoon salt
- 1 teaspoon ground cinnamon
- 1/2 teaspoon ground nutmeg
- 1/4 teaspoon ground cloves
- 1/4 teaspoon ground ginger
- 1/2 cup unsalted butter, melted
- 1 cup canned pumpkin puree
- 2 large eggs
- 1 teaspoon vanilla extract
- 3/4 cup brown sugar
- 1/4 cup granulated sugar
- 1/2 cup milk

Optional:

- chopped nuts, raisins, or chocolate chips for topping

Time of preparation:

- Preparation Time: 15 minutes
- Baking Time: 20-25 minutes
- Total Time: 35-40 minutes

Procedure:

- Set a muffin tin with paper liners or coat the cups with nonstick cooking spray and preheat the oven to 375°F (190°C).
- In a large mixing bowl, whisk together the flour, baking powder, baking soda, salt, cinnamon, nutmeg, cloves, and ginger until well combined.
- In another bowl, mix together the melted butter, pumpkin puree, eggs, vanilla extract, brown sugar, and granulated sugar until smooth.
- Stirring until just blended, gradually add the wet components to the dry ingredients. Do not overmix.
- Stir in the milk until the batter is smooth and evenly mixed.
- Pour the mixture into the muffin tins, filling each one to approximately two thirds of the way to the top.
- If desired, sprinkle the tops of the muffins with chopped nuts, raisins, or chocolate chips for added flavor and texture.
- A toothpick put into the centre of a muffin should come out clean after 20 to 25 minutes of baking in a preheated oven.
- Remove the muffins from the oven and allow them to cool in the muffin tin for 5 minutes before transferring them to a wire rack to cool completely.

Nutritional Value per Serving:

- Calories: 200
- Total Fat: 8g
- Saturated Fat: 5g
- Cholesterol: 45mg
- Sodium: 200mg
- Total Carbohydrate: 30g
- Dietary Fiber: 1g
- Sugars: 16g
- Protein: 3g

Health Benefits:

- Pumpkin is rich in vitamin A, fiber, and antioxidants.
- The spices used in the muffins provide additional antioxidants and anti-inflammatory properties.
- By using whole wheat flour or reducing the amount of sugar, you can make the muffins even healthier.

Packaging and Storing:

- After the muffins are totally cold, you can keep them at room temperature for up to three days in an airtight container.
- For longer storage, individually wrap the muffins in plastic wrap and freeze them in a freezer-safe bag for up to 3 months.

Precautions and Safety:

- Ensure the muffins are fully cooled before storing to prevent moisture buildup and mold growth.
- Be cautious not to overmix the batter, as this can result in dense and tough muffins.

Post-Caution:

- Thaw frozen muffins in the refrigerator overnight or microwave them for a quick snack.
- Avoid consuming muffins that show signs of mold or spoilage.

# Autumn Harvest Soup

Ingredients:

- 2 tablespoons olive oil
- 1 onion, diced
- 2 cloves garlic, minced
- 2 carrots, peeled and diced
- 2 stalks celery, diced
- 1 sweet potato, peeled and diced
- 1 butternut squash, peeled, seeded, and diced
- 4 cups vegetable broth
- 1 teaspoon dried thyme
- 1/2 teaspoon ground cinnamon
- Salt and pepper to taste

Optional:

- 1/2 cup heavy cream or coconut milk for added creaminess

Optional toppings:

- chopped fresh parsley, croutons, or a dollop of sour cream

Preparation Time:

- Preparation Time: 15 minutes
- Cooking Time: 30 minutes
- Total Time: 45 minutes

Procedure:

- Warm up the olive oil in a big pot over medium heat.
- Add diced onion, garlic, carrots, and celery. Sauté until onions are translucent and vegetables are tender, about 5-7 minutes.
- Add diced sweet potato and butternut squash to the pot. Cook for a another five minutes, stirring now and then.
- Pour in vegetable broth, ensuring that the vegetables are covered. Bring to a boil, then reduce heat to low and simmer for 20-25 minutes, or until the vegetables are soft and cooked through.
- Puree the soup with an immersion blender until it's creamy and smooth. Alternatively, pour the soup into a blender in batches and process until smooth.
- Be cautious when blending hot liquids.
- Stir in dried thyme, ground cinnamon, salt, and pepper to taste. Adjust seasoning as needed.
- If desired, add heavy cream or coconut milk to the soup for added creaminess. Stir until well combined.
- Allow the soup to simmer for an additional 5 minutes to allow flavors to meld.
- Serve hot, garnished with optional toppings like chopped fresh parsley, croutons, or a dollop of sour cream.

Nutritional Value per Serving:

- Calories: 200
- Total Fat: 8g
- Saturated Fat: 2g
- Cholesterol: 10mg
- Sodium: 600mg
- Total Carbohydrate: 30g
- Dietary Fiber: 6g
- Sugars: 10g

- Protein: 4g

Health Benefits:

- abundant in minerals, vitamins, and antioxidants derived from a range of vegetables.
- It's a good choice for managing weight because it's low in calories and fat.
- The soup is rich in dietary fiber, promoting digestive health and satiety.

Packaging and Storing:

- Before storing the soup in sealed jars, let it cool fully.
- Keep refrigerated for a maximum of four to five days.
- Freeze the soup for up to three months in freezer-safe containers for extended storage.

Precautions and Safety:

- Be careful when handling hot soup and using the blender to avoid burns.
- Use caution when pureeing hot liquids to prevent splattering.

Post-Caution:

- When reheating the soup, ensure it reaches a safe internal temperature of 165°F (74°C) to prevent foodborne illness.
- Discard any leftover soup that has been left at room temperature for more than 2 hours to avoid bacterial contamination.

# Chapter 4

# Winter Warmers

# Roasted Root Vegetable Medley

Ingredients:

- Three big carrots, cut into bits after peeling
- Peel and chop two medium parsnips into pieces.
- Peel and chop two medium sweet potatoes into pieces.
- One large beetroot, chopped into bits after peeling
- One red onion, sliced into wedges after peeling
- 4 cloves garlic, minced
- 3 tablespoons olive oil
- 1 teaspoon dried thyme
- 1 teaspoon dried rosemary
- Salt and pepper to taste

Time of preparation:

- Preparation Time: 15 minutes
- Cooking Time: 30 minutes
- Total Time: 45 minutes

Procedure:

- Preheat the oven to 400°F (200°C).
- In a large mixing bowl, combine all the chopped vegetables and minced garlic.
- After drizzling the veggies with olive oil, toss to coat them evenly.
- Sprinkle dried thyme, dried rosemary, salt, and pepper over the vegetables, and toss again to distribute the seasonings evenly.
- Arrange the vegetables in a single layer on a parchment paper-lined baking sheet.

- Roast in the preheated oven for 25-30 minutes, or until the vegetables are tender and slightly caramelized, stirring halfway through cooking.
- Once roasted, remove from the oven and let cool slightly before serving.

Tips and Tricks:

- For consistent cooking, chop the vegetables into uniform pieces.
- Don't overcrowd the baking sheet to allow the vegetables to roast evenly.
- For extra flavor, you can sprinkle some grated Parmesan cheese over the roasted vegetables before serving.

Nutritional Value per Serving (approximate):

- Calories: 180
- Fat: 7g
- Carbohydrates: 28g
- Fiber: 6g
- Protein: 3g

Health Benefits:

- Rich in minerals, vitamins, and fibre; contains potassium, vitamin C, and vitamin A
- Low in calories and fat, making it a healthy side dish option.
- The combination of root vegetables provides a variety of antioxidants that promote overall health.

Packaging and Storing:

- Any leftovers can be kept for up to three or four days in the refrigerator in an airtight container.
- Before serving, reheat in the microwave or oven until well heated.

Precautions and Post-Caution:

- Be cautious when handling hot baking sheets and roasted vegetables to avoid burns.
- Check the tenderness of the vegetables before removing them from the oven to ensure they are cooked through.

Safety Caution:

- Always use oven mitts when handling hot trays or dishes.
- Supervise children when they are helping with preparation or serving to prevent accidents.
- Enjoy your delicious and nutritious Roasted Root Vegetable Medley!

## Creamy Potato Leek Soup

Ingredients:

- Three large leeks, cleaned and cut, with just the white and light green sections
- 4 medium potatoes, peeled and diced
- 2 tablespoons butter
- 4 cups vegetable or chicken broth
- 1 cup heavy cream
- Salt and pepper to taste
- Chopped chives or parsley for garnish (optional)

Time of preparation

- Preparation Time: 15 minutes
- Cooking Time: 30 minutes
- Total Time: 45 minutes

Procedure:

- Melt the butter in a big pot over a medium heat.
- Sliced leeks should be added to the pot and cooked for five to seven minutes, stirring now and then, until they are tender and transparent.
- Pour the chicken or vegetable broth into the pot along with the cubed potatoes.
- Bring the mixture to a boil, then reduce the heat to low, cover, and simmer for 20-25 minutes, or until the potatoes are tender.
- Puree the soup with an immersion blender until it's creamy and smooth. Alternately, pour the soup back into the pot after transferring it in batches to a blender and blending until smooth.
- Add the heavy cream and taste and adjust the seasoning with salt and pepper.
- . Alternatively, transfer the soup in batches to a blender and blend until smooth, then return to the pot.
- Continue to cook the soup for another 5 minutes, stirring occasionally, until heated through.
- Serve hot, garnished with chopped chives or parsley if desired.

Tips and Tricks:

- Be sure to thoroughly clean the leeks as they often contain dirt and grit between the layers.
- For a richer flavor, you can use half-and-half or whole milk instead of heavy cream, although the soup won't be as creamy.
- Feel free to add additional seasonings such as garlic powder, thyme, or bay leaves for extra flavor.

Nutritional Value per Serving (approximate):

- Calories: 250
- Fat: 15g
- Carbohydrates: 25g

- Fiber: 3g
- Protein: 4g

Health Benefits:

- Leeks are a good source of manganese, folate, and vitamins A, C, and K.
- Potatoes provide a good source of vitamin C, potassium, and dietary fiber.
- This soup is creamy and satisfying while being relatively low in calories.

Packaging and Storing:

- Let the soup cool fully before putting it in sealed jars.
- Keep refrigerated for a maximum of three to four days.
- Reheat gently on the stovetop, stirring occasionally until warmed through.

Precautions and Post-Caution:

- Be cautious when blending hot soup to avoid splattering and burns.
- Make sure the soup is not boiling hot when serving to avoid burns.

Safety Caution:

- Always use caution when working with hot liquids and appliances in the kitchen.
- Keep children away from hot stovetops and blenders to prevent accidents.
- Enjoy your comforting and delicious Creamy Potato Leek Soup!

# Cranberry Orange Bread Pudding

Ingredients:

- 6 cups of stale bread, cut into cubes (use French bread or brioche for best results)
- 1 cup dried cranberries
- Zest of 1 orange
- 4 large eggs
- 2 cups whole milk
- 1/2 cup granulated sugar
- 1 teaspoon vanilla extract
- 1/2 teaspoon ground cinnamon
- Pinch of salt
- Butter for greasing the baking dish

Time of preparation

- Preparation Time: 15 minutes
- Baking Time: 45 minutes
- Total Time: 1 hour

Procedure:

- Preheat the oven to 350°F (175°C). Apply butter grease to a 9 × 13-inch baking dish.
- In a large mixing bowl, combine the bread cubes and dried cranberries.
- In another bowl, whisk together the eggs, whole milk, granulated sugar, vanilla extract, orange zest, cinnamon, and a pinch of salt until well combined.
- Pour the egg mixture over the bread cubes and cranberries. Make sure the mixture coats all of the bread cubes by giving them a gentle toss.
- Allow the bread to absorb the liquid by letting the mixture sit for approximately ten minutes.
- Transfer the bread pudding mixture into the prepared baking dish, spreading it out evenly.
- Bake in the preheated oven for 45-50 minutes, or until the top is golden brown and the pudding is set.
- Before serving, take it out of the oven and allow it to cool for a few minutes.

Tips and Tricks:

- Use stale bread as it will absorb the custard mixture better without becoming too soggy.
- You can substitute the dried cranberries with raisins or chopped dried apricots if desired.
- For added flavor, you can sprinkle some chopped nuts like pecans or walnuts on top before baking.

Nutritional Value per Serving (approximate):

- Calories: 250
- Fat: 8g
- Carbohydrates: 38g
- Fiber: 2g
- Protein: 7g

Health Benefits:

- Cranberries are rich in antioxidants and vitamin C, which can help boost the immune system.
- Oranges provide vitamin C and fiber, promoting overall health and digestion.

- While bread pudding is not a low-calorie dessert, it can be enjoyed in moderation as a comforting treat.

Packaging and Storing:

- Allow the bread pudding to cool completely before storing.
- Any leftovers can be kept for up to three or four days in the refrigerator in an airtight container.
- Reheat individual servings in the microwave or oven until warmed through before serving.

Precautions and Post-Caution:

- Be careful when handling hot baking dishes and utensils.
- Allow the bread pudding to cool slightly before serving to prevent burns from hot steam.

Safety Caution:

- Ensure the bread pudding is cooked through by inserting a knife into the center; it should come out clean.
- Always use oven mitts when handling hot dishes and pans.
- Enjoy your delightful Cranberry Orange Bread Pudding!

# Hearty Beef Stew

Ingredients:

- 2 pounds stewing beef, cut into 1-inch cubes
- 3 tablespoons all-purpose flour
- Salt and pepper to taste
- 2 tablespoons olive oil
- 1 large onion, chopped
- 3 cloves garlic, minced
- 4 carrots, peeled and sliced
- 4 celery stalks, sliced
- 2 large potatoes, peeled and diced
- 4 cups beef broth
- 1 cup red wine (optional)
- 2 bay leaves
- 1 teaspoon dried thyme
- 1 teaspoon dried rosemary
- Chopped fresh parsley for garnish (optional)

Time of preparation:

- Preparation Time: 20 minutes
- Cooking Time: 2 hours
- Total Time: 2 hours 20 minutes

Procedure:

- In a large bowl, combine the cubed beef with flour, salt, and pepper, tossing to coat evenly.
- In a large pot or Dutch oven, heat the olive oil over medium-high heat. In batches, add the beef cubes and sauté them until they are browned all over. Take out and place aside.
- Add minced garlic and chopped onions to the same saucepan. Simmer until garlic is aromatic and onions are transparent.
- Return the browned beef to the pot. Add sliced carrots, celery, and diced potatoes.
- Pour in beef broth and red wine (if using). Add bay leaves, dried thyme, and dried rosemary.
- After bringing the mixture to a boil, turn down the heat. . Cover and simmer for 1.5 to 2 hours, or until the beef is tender and the vegetables are cooked through.
- Season with additional salt and pepper to taste. Remove bay leaves before serving.
- Garnish with chopped fresh parsley, if desired.

Tips and Tricks:

- Choose tough cuts of beef like chuck or round for stewing, as they become tender and flavorful when cooked slowly.
- Browning the beef before stewing adds depth of flavor to the dish.
- You can add other vegetables like peas, green beans, or mushrooms according to your preference.

Nutritional Value per Serving (approximate):

- Calories: 350
- Fat: 15g
- Carbohydrates: 20g
- Fiber: 4g
- Protein: 30g

Health Benefits:

- Beef stew is rich in protein, which is essential for muscle repair and growth.
- The vegetables in the stew provide vitamins, minerals, and fiber, promoting overall health and digestion.
- Homemade beef stew can be lower in sodium and fat compared to store-bought versions, making it a healthier option.

Packaging and Storing:

- Allow the stew to cool completely before transferring to airtight containers.
- Keep refrigerated for a maximum of three to four days.
- Stew can also be frozen to extend its shelf life. Let cool fully before transferring to freezer-safe bags or containers. Date the label, then freeze for a maximum of three months.

Precautions and Post-Caution:

- Check the beef stew for any bones or cartilage before serving to avoid choking hazards.
- Ensure the stew is heated through before serving leftovers.

Safety Caution:

- Use caution when working with hot liquids and appliances in the kitchen.
- Keep children away from hot stovetops and utensils to prevent accidents.
- Enjoy the comforting and delicious Hearty Beef Stew!

# Chapter 5

# Holiday Specials

# Thanksgiving Feast: A Seasonal Spread

Ingredients:

For the Turkey:

- 1 whole turkey (12-15 pounds)
- Salt and pepper to taste
- 1 cup butter, softened
- 4 cloves garlic, minced
- 2 tablespoons fresh rosemary, chopped
- 2 tablespoons fresh thyme, chopped
- 2 tablespoons fresh sage, chopped
- 2 onions, quartered
- 4 carrots, chopped
- 4 stalks celery, chopped

For the Stuffing:

- 1 loaf bread, cubed and toasted
- 2 onions, diced
- 4 stalks celery, diced
- 4 cloves garlic, minced
- 2 apples, diced
- 1 cup dried cranberries
- 1 cup chopped pecans

- 2 tablespoons fresh sage, chopped
- 2 tablespoons fresh thyme, chopped
- 2 cups chicken broth
- Salt and pepper to taste
- For the Mashed Potatoes:
- 5 pounds potatoes, peeled and cubed
- 1 cup milk
- ½ cup butter
- Salt and pepper to taste
- Chopped chives for garnish

For the Gravy:

- Pan drippings from the turkey
- ¼ cup all-purpose flour
- 2 cups chicken broth
- Salt and pepper to taste

For the Green Bean Casserole:

- 2 pounds green beans, trimmed
- 1 can cream of mushroom soup
- 1 cup milk
- 1 teaspoon soy sauce
- ½ teaspoon black pepper
- 1 cup French fried onions

For the Cranberry Sauce:

- 1 bag fresh cranberries
- 1 cup orange juice
- 1 cup sugar
- Zest of 1 orange

For the Pumpkin Pie:

- 1 ½ cups pumpkin puree
- ¾ cup sugar

- 1 teaspoon ground cinnamon
- ½ teaspoon ground ginger
- ¼ teaspoon ground cloves
- ¼ teaspoon ground nutmeg
- 2 eggs
- 1 cup evaporated milk
- 1 pie crust (store-bought or homemade)

### Time of preparation

- (1-2 days before)

### Procedures:

- Thaw the turkey in the refrigerator if frozen.
- Cube and toast the bread for the stuffing.
- Prepare the cranberry sauce and store it in the refrigerator.

### Day of Thanksgiving:

- Preheat the oven to 325°F (165°C).
- After rinsing, blot the turkey dry with paper towels.
- Use salt and pepper to season the turkey from the inside out..
- In a small bowl, mix together butter, garlic, rosemary, thyme, and sage.
- Loosen the skin of the turkey and rub the butter mixture under the skin.
- Stuff the turkey with quartered onions, chopped carrots, and celery.
- Roast the turkey in the preheated oven for 3-4 hours or until the internal temperature reaches 165°F (75°C).
- While the turkey is roasting, prepare the stuffing, mashed potatoes, gravy, green bean casserole, and pumpkin pie according to their respective recipes.

### Tips and Tricks:

- Thaw the turkey in the refrigerator, allowing 24 hours for every 4-5 pounds of turkey.
- To make sure the turkey is cooked through, use a meat thermometer.
- To allow the liquids to redistribute, let the turkey rest for at least 20 to 30 minutes before carving.

- Make the gravy using the drippings from the turkey for maximum flavor.
- To save time, prepare some dishes in advance and reheat them before serving.

Nutritional Value per Serving:

- The nutritional value varies depending on the portion size and ingredients used. However, traditional Thanksgiving dishes are often rich in protein, carbohydrates, vitamins, and minerals.

Health Benefits:

- Turkey is a lean source of protein and contains vitamins and minerals like niacin, vitamin B6, selenium, and zinc.
- Cranberries are rich in antioxidants and may have benefits for heart health.
- Green beans are rich in fibre, vitamins, and minerals and low in calories.
- Pumpkin is high in fiber, vitamins A and C, and antioxidants.

Packaging and Storing:

- Store leftovers in airtight containers and refrigerate them within 2 hours of cooking.
- You can freeze leftovers for up to three months or keep them in the fridge for three to four days..

Precautions and Post-Caution:

- Handle raw turkey carefully to prevent cross-contamination.
- Thoroughly cook the turkey to kill any harmful bacteria.
- Reheat leftovers to an internal temperature of 165°F (75°C) before consuming.

Safety Caution:

- Always wash hands, utensils, and surfaces thoroughly before and after handling raw poultry.
- Use separate cutting boards for raw poultry and other ingredients to avoid contamination.
- Perishable items should be kept chilled until needed.

# Festive Winter Cocktails

Ingredients:

Spiced Mulled Wine:

- 1 bottle red wine
- 1 orange, sliced
- 1/4 cup honey or sugar
- 4 whole cloves
- 2 cinnamon sticks
- 2 star anise
- 1/4 teaspoon nutmeg

Optional :

- brandy or rum for extra warmth

Cranberry Moscow Mule:

- 2 oz vodka
- 1 oz cranberry juice
- 1/2 oz lime juice
- Ginger beer
- Fresh cranberries and rosemary for garnish

Winter Wonderland White Russian:

- 2 oz vodka
- 1 oz coffee liqueur (e.g., Kahlua)
- 1 oz cream or milk
- Crushed ice
- Cinnamon sticks for garnish

Hot Buttered Rum:

- 2 oz dark rum
- 2 tablespoons unsalted butter, softened
- 1 tablespoon brown sugar
- Pinch of cinnamon
- Pinch of nutmeg
- Hot water

Time of Preparation:

- Preparation time varies depending on the complexity of the cocktail, but most can be prepared within 5-10 minutes.

Procedures:

Spiced Mulled Wine:

- In a large saucepan, combine red wine, orange slices, honey or sugar, cloves, cinnamon sticks, star anise, and nutmeg.
- Heat over low-medium heat until warm, but not boiling, stirring occasionally.
- Once warmed through, strain the mulled wine into mugs and serve hot. Optionally, add a splash of brandy or rum to each mug.

Cranberry Moscow Mule:

- Fill a copper mug with ice.
- Add vodka, cranberry juice, and lime juice.
- Top with ginger beer and stir gently.
- Add some fresh cranberries and a rosemary leaf as garnish.

Winter Wonderland White Russian:

- Fill a glass with crushed ice.
- Pour in vodka and coffee liqueur.
- Top with cream or milk and stir gently.
- Garnish with a cinnamon stick for added winter flair.

Hot Buttered Rum:

- In a heatproof mug, combine dark rum, softened butter, brown sugar, cinnamon, and nutmeg.
- Fill the mug with hot water and stir until the butter and sugar are melted and well combined.
- Optionally, garnish with a cinnamon stick or sprinkle of nutmeg.

Tips and Tricks:

- Choose quality ingredients for the best flavor.
- Adjust sweetness and spice levels to suit personal taste preferences.
- Use freshly squeezed citrus juice for optimal freshness.
- Garnish cocktails with seasonal fruits, herbs, or spices for visual appeal.
- Experiment with different spirits and mixers to create unique flavor combinations.

Nutritional Value per Serving:

- The nutritional value varies depending on the ingredients used in each cocktail. However, most winter cocktails are higher in calories and sugar due to the inclusion of alcohol and sweet mixers.

Health Benefits:

- Moderate consumption of red wine may have cardiovascular benefits due to its antioxidant content.
- Cranberry juice is rich in vitamin C and antioxidants, which may support immune health.
- While cocktails can be enjoyed in moderation as part of a balanced lifestyle, excessive alcohol consumption can have adverse health effects.

Packaging and Storing:

- Cocktails should be served immediately after preparation for the best taste and quality.
- Leftover ingredients, such as mulled wine mix or infused syrups, can be stored in airtight containers in the refrigerator for future use.

Precautions and Post-Caution:

- Enjoy cocktails responsibly and be mindful of alcohol consumption.
- Never drink and drive. Plan a different mode of transportation if you plan to drink.
- Be cautious when handling hot liquids to avoid burns or spills.

Safety Caution:

- Keep cocktail ingredients out of reach of children and pets.
- Use caution when using open flames, such as when lighting garnishes or heating ingredients.
- Drink responsibly and know your limits to prevent alcohol-related accidents or injuries.

# Roast Turkey with Cranberry Sauce

Ingredients:

For the Turkey:

- 1 whole turkey (12-15 pounds)
- Salt and pepper to taste
- 1 cup butter, softened
- 4 cloves garlic, minced
- 2 tablespoons fresh rosemary, chopped
- 2 tablespoons fresh thyme, chopped
- 2 tablespoons fresh sage, chopped
- 2 onions, quartered
- 4 carrots, chopped
- 4 stalks celery, chopped

For the Cranberry Sauce:

- 1 bag fresh cranberries
- 1 cup orange juice
- 1 cup sugar
- Zest of 1 orange

## Time of Preparation:

- Preparing and roasting the turkey typically takes around 3-4 hours, depending on the size of the turkey.

## Procedure:

- Preheat the oven to 325°F (165°C).
- After rinsing, blot the turkey dry with paper towels.
- Use salt and pepper to season the turkey from the inside out.
- In a small bowl, mix together butter, garlic, rosemary, thyme, and sage.
- Loosen the skin of the turkey and rub the butter mixture under the skin.
- Stuff the turkey with quartered onions, chopped carrots, and celery.

## Roasting the Turkey:

- Arrange the turkey, breast side up, on a roasting pan rack.
- Cover the turkey with foil and cook it at a temperature of 165°F (75°C) for approximately 15 minutes for every pound.
- In order to allow the skin to brown during the final thirty minutes of cooking, remove the foil.

## Making the Cranberry Sauce:

- In a saucepan, combine fresh cranberries, orange juice, sugar, and orange zest.
- Bring to a boil over medium heat, then reduce the heat and simmer for about 10-15 minutes, or until the cranberries burst and the sauce thickens.
- Remove from heat and let cool before serving.

## Tips and Tricks:

- Thaw the turkey in the refrigerator if frozen, allowing 24 hours for every 4-5 pounds of turkey.
- Make sure the turkey is cooked through by using a meat thermometer to check the internal temperature, which should be 165°F (75°C).
- To allow the liquids to redistribute, let the turkey rest for at least 20 to 30 minutes before carving.
- Make the cranberry sauce ahead of time to allow the flavors to meld together.

Nutritional Value per Serving:

- The nutritional value varies depending on the portion size and ingredients used. However, roast turkey is a good source of protein, vitamins, and minerals, while cranberries are rich in antioxidants and vitamin C.

Health Benefits:

- Lean proteins like turkey can help with muscle growth and repair.
- Cranberries contain antioxidants that may help reduce inflammation and promote urinary tract health.

Packaging and Storing:

- Store leftover turkey and cranberry sauce in separate airtight containers in the refrigerator.
- Leftover turkey can be stored in the refrigerator for 3-4 days or frozen for longer storage.
- Cranberry sauce can be refrigerated for up to a week.

Precautions and Post-Caution:

- Handle raw turkey carefully to prevent cross-contamination.
- Thoroughly cook the turkey to kill any harmful bacteria.
- Refrigerate leftovers promptly after the meal to prevent foodborne illness.

Safety Caution:

- Always wash hands, utensils, and surfaces thoroughly before and after handling raw poultry.
- Use separate cutting boards for raw poultry and other ingredients to avoid contamination.
- Ensure the turkey reaches the proper internal temperature to ensure food safety.

# Christmas Morning Breakfast Casserole

Ingredients:

- 8 slices bread, cubed
- 1 pound breakfast sausage, cooked and crumbled
- 1 cup shredded cheddar cheese
- 6 eggs
- 2 cups milk
- 1 teaspoon mustard powder
- Salt and pepper to taste

Optional toppings:

- sliced green onions, diced tomatoes, cooked bacon bits

Time of Preparation:

- The preparation time for this Christmas Morning Breakfast Casserole is approximately 20 minutes, with an additional baking time of around 1 hour

Procedures:

- Preheat the oven to 350°F (175°C).
- Grease a 9x13 inch baking dish.
- Cube the bread slices and layer them evenly in the baking dish.
- Cook and crumble the breakfast sausage.

- Sprinkle the cooked sausage over the bread cubes.
- Sprinkle shredded cheddar cheese evenly over the sausage layer.

Preparing the Egg Mixture:

- Beat eggs, milk, mustard powder, salt, and pepper in a mixing bowl until thoroughly blended..
- Pour the egg mixture evenly over the bread, sausage, and cheese layers.

Baking:

- Bake the baking dish for forty-five minutes with the foil covering it.
- Remove the foil and bake for an additional 15 minutes, or until the casserole is set and golden brown on top.

Serve:

- Before slicing, allow the casserole to cool for a few minutes.Serve hot, garnished with optional toppings if desired.

Tips and Tricks:

- For improved egg mixture absorption, use day-old bread.
- Customize the casserole by adding your favorite ingredients such as diced bell peppers, mushrooms, or spinach.
- Allow the casserole to rest for a few minutes before serving to set and prevent it from falling apart when sliced.
- The casserole should be made the night before and chilled. For a stress-free morning meal, bake it in the morning.

Nutritional Value per Serving:

- The nutritional value per serving of this breakfast casserole will vary based on portion size and specific ingredients used. However, it typically provides a good balance of carbohydrates, protein, and fats.

Health Benefits:

- Eggs are rich in protein, vitamins, and minerals, including vitamin D and choline.

- Sausage adds protein and flavor to the dish, but opt for leaner varieties to reduce saturated fat content.
- Incorporating whole grain bread can increase fiber intake, promoting digestive health and providing sustained energy.

Packaging and Storing:

- Allow any leftover casserole to cool completely before transferring it to an airtight container.
- The casserole can be kept in the fridge for up to three days.
- Reheat individual servings in the microwave or oven until heated through before serving.

Precautions and Post-Caution:

- Ensure that the sausage is fully cooked before adding it to the casserole to prevent foodborne illness.
- Refrigerate leftovers promptly after serving to minimize the risk of bacterial growth.

Safety Caution:

- Use caution when handling hot dishes and appliances.
- Avoid cross-contamination by cleaning and sanitizing utensils and surfaces after handling raw meat.
- Always wash hands thoroughly before and after preparing food to prevent the spread of bacteria.

# Chapter 6

# Quick And Easy Weeknight Meals

# One-Pan Balsamic Chicken with Vegetables

Ingredients:

- 4 boneless, skinless chicken breasts
- 2 tablespoons olive oil
- 1/4 cup balsamic vinegar
- 3 cloves garlic, minced
- 1 teaspoon dried oregano
- 1 teaspoon dried thyme
- Salt and pepper to taste
- 1 red bell pepper, sliced
- 1 yellow bell pepper, sliced
- 1 red onion, sliced
- 1 cup cherry tomatoes
- Fresh parsley for garnish

Time of preparation;

- Preparation Time: 15 minutes
- Cooking: 25 minutes
- Total Time: 40 minutes

Procedure:

- Preheat the oven to 400°F (200°C).
- In a small bowl, whisk together olive oil, balsamic vinegar, minced garlic, dried oregano, dried thyme, salt, and pepper.
- Place the chicken breasts in a large ziplock bag or a shallow dish, and pour half of the balsamic mixture over them. Let give it a minimum of ten minutes to marinate.
- In an oven-safe skillet, preheat the heat to medium-high. When the chicken breasts are added, marinade them for two to three minutes on each side, or until browned.
- After taking the chicken out of the skillet, set it aside.
- Add the sliced bell peppers and onion to the skillet, and cook for 4-5 minutes until they start to soften.
- Return the chicken to the skillet, along with cherry tomatoes, and pour the remaining balsamic mixture over everything.
- Place the skillet in the oven that has been prepared, and bake for 15 to 20 minutes, or until the vegetables are soft and the chicken is cooked through.
- Garnish with fresh parsley before serving.

Nutritional Value (per serving):

- Calories: 280 kcal
- Protein: 28g
- Fat: 10g
- Carbohydrates: 18g
- Fiber: 4g
- Sugar: 10g

Health Benefits:

- High in protein which helps in muscle building and repair.
- Rich in antioxidants from vegetables, aiding in reducing inflammation and preventing oxidative stress.
- Balanced mix of macronutrients, suitable for a healthy diet.

Packaging and Storing:

- Allow the dish to cool completely before storing.
- Remaining food can be kept in the refrigerator for up to three days if it is sealed tightly.
- Reheat in the oven or microwave until well warm.
- Precautions:
- Ensure chicken is cooked thoroughly to avoid foodborne illness.
- Use separate cutting boards and utensils for raw chicken and vegetables to prevent cross-contamination.
- After handling raw chicken, properly wash your hands and all surfaces.

Safety Caution:

- Use oven mitts when handling hot skillet and removing from the oven.
- Keep children and pets away from the kitchen during cooking to prevent accidents.
- Check the internal temperature of the chicken using a meat thermometer to ensure it reaches 165°F (75°C) for safety.

# Quinoa Primavera Bowl

Ingredients:

- 1 cup quinoa, rinsed
- 2 cups vegetable broth or water
- 1 tablespoon olive oil
- 2 cloves garlic, minced
- 1 small onion, diced
- 1 red bell pepper, diced
- 1 yellow bell pepper, diced
- 1 cup cherry tomatoes, halved
- 1 cup broccoli florets
- 1 cup sliced mushrooms
- Salt and pepper to taste
- 1/4 cup grated Parmesan cheese (optional)
- Fresh parsley or basil for garnish

Time of preparation:

- Preparation Time: 10 minutes
- Cooking: 20 minutes
- Total Time: 30 minutes

Procedure:

- In a medium saucepan, combine quinoa and vegetable broth (or water). Bring to a boil, then reduce heat to low, cover, and simmer for 15-20 minutes, or until quinoa is cooked and liquid is absorbed. Take it off the heat and leave it covered for five minutes.
- Heat the olive oil in a big skillet over medium heat while the quinoa cooks.
- Add minced garlic and diced onion, and cook until softened, about 2-3 minutes.
- Add diced bell peppers, cherry tomatoes, broccoli florets, and sliced mushrooms to the skillet. Cook, stirring occasionally, for 5-7 minutes, or until vegetables are tender but still crisp.
- To taste, add salt and pepper to the vegetables.
- To assemble the bowls, divide cooked quinoa among serving bowls, and top with the sautéed vegetables.
- If desired, sprinkle grated Parmesan cheese over the top of each bowl.
- Garnish with fresh parsley or basil before serving.

Nutritional Value (per serving):

- Calories: 320 kcal
- Protein: 10g
- Fat: 8g
- Carbohydrates: 50g
- Fiber: 8g
- Sugar: 6g

Health Benefits:

- Quinoa has all nine of the essential amino acids, making it a complete protein source.
- Rich in fibre, which facilitates digestion and increases feelings of fullness.
- Packed with vitamins and minerals from a variety of vegetables, contributing to overall health and well-being.

Packaging and Storing:

- Allow the Quinoa Primavera Bowl to cool completely before storing.
- Remaining food can be kept in the refrigerator for up to three days if it is sealed tightly.

- Before serving, reheat in the microwave or on the hob until thoroughly warm.

Precautions:

- Rinse quinoa thoroughly before cooking to remove any bitter taste caused by saponins.
- Be cautious when handling hot pans and boiling liquids to prevent burns.
- Use fresh vegetables and ingredients to maximize flavor and nutritional value.

Safety Caution:

- Ensure quinoa is cooked properly to avoid any risk of foodborne illness.
- Keep knives and cutting boards clean and sanitized to prevent cross-contamination between raw vegetables and cooked quinoa.
- Store leftovers promptly and refrigerate to prevent spoilage.

# 30-Minute Shrimp and Broccoli Stir-Fry

Ingredients:

- 1 pound large shrimp, peeled and deveined
- 2 cups broccoli florets
- 2 tablespoons soy sauce
- 1 tablespoon oyster sauce
- 1 tablespoon hoisin sauce
- 1 tablespoon sesame oil
- 2 cloves garlic, minced
- 1 teaspoon fresh ginger, grated
- 2 tablespoons vegetable oil
- Cooked rice or noodles for serving
- Garnish with chopped green onions and sesame seeds.

Time of preparation:

- Preparation Time :15 minutes
- Cooking: 15 minutes
- Total Time: 30 minutes

Procedure:

- In a small bowl, mix together soy sauce, oyster sauce, hoisin sauce, sesame oil, minced garlic, and grated ginger. Set aside.

- Heat vegetable oil in a large skillet or wok over medium-high heat.
- Add shrimp to the skillet and cook for 2-3 minutes on each side until pink and opaque. Take out and place aside the prawns from the skillet.
- In the same skillet, add broccoli florets and stir-fry for 3-4 minutes until tender-crisp.
- Return the cooked shrimp to the skillet, and pour the sauce mixture over the shrimp and broccoli.
- Stir well to coat everything evenly and cook for an additional 1-2 minutes until heated through.
- Serve the shrimp and broccoli stir-fry over cooked rice or noodles.
- Before serving, garnish with sliced green onions and sesame seeds..

Nutritional Value (per serving):

- Calories: 280 kcal
- Protein: 25g
- Fat: 12g
- Carbohydrates: 18g
- Fiber: 3g
- Sugar: 2g

Health Benefits:

- Shrimp is low in calories and rich in protein, making it a healthy seafood option.
- Rich in vitamins, minerals, and antioxidants, broccoli promotes general health and wellbeing.
- This dish is low in carbohydrates and high in protein, making it suitable for those watching their carb intake.

Packaging and Storing:

- Allow the shrimp and broccoli stir-fry to cool slightly before storing.
- Remaining food can be kept in the refrigerator for up to two days if it is sealed tightly.
- Before serving, reheat in the microwave or on the hob until thoroughly warm.

Precautions:

- Thaw shrimp properly if using frozen shrimp before cooking to ensure even cooking.
- Be cautious when handling hot pans and oil to prevent burns.
- Adjust the amount of soy sauce and other sauces according to your taste preferences and dietary restrictions.

Safety Caution:

- Ensure shrimp is cooked thoroughly to avoid any risk of foodborne illness.
- Use separate utensils and cutting boards for raw shrimp and vegetables to prevent cross-contamination.
- Store leftovers promptly and refrigerate to prevent spoilage.

# Stir-Fried Noodles with Tofu and Vegetables

Ingredients:

- 8 oz (225g) dried noodles (such as rice noodles or udon noodles)
- 8 oz (225 g) diced and pressed firm tofu
- 2 tablespoons soy sauce
- 1 tablespoon sesame oil
- 2 tablespoons vegetable oil
- 3 cloves garlic, minced
- 1 teaspoon fresh ginger, grated
- 1 red bell pepper, thinly sliced
- 1 carrot, julienned
- 2 cups broccoli florets
- 1 cup sliced mushrooms
- 2 green onions, sliced
- Salt and pepper to taste
- Sesame seeds for garnish (optional)
- Fresh cilantro or parsley for garnish (optional)

Time of preparation :

- Preparation Time: 20 minutes
- Cooking: 15 minutes

- Total Time: 35 minutes

Procedure:

- Noodles should be cooked as directed on the package until they are al dente. . Drain and set aside.
- In a small bowl, mix together soy sauce and sesame oil. Set aside.
- Heat vegetable oil in a large skillet or wok over medium-high heat.
- Add cubed tofu to the skillet and cook until golden brown on all sides, about 5-7 minutes. Remove tofu from the skillet and set aside.
- In the same skillet, add minced garlic and grated ginger. Cook for 1-2 minutes until fragrant.
- Add sliced bell pepper, julienned carrot, broccoli florets, and sliced mushrooms to the skillet. Stir-fry for 5-7 minutes until vegetables are tender-crisp.
- Return the cooked tofu to the skillet, along with cooked noodles and the soy sauce mixture. Toss everything together until well combined and heated through.
- Season with salt and pepper to taste.
- Garnish with sliced green onions, sesame seeds, and fresh cilantro or parsley before serving.

Nutritional Value (per serving):

- Calories: 350 kcal
- Protein: 15g
- Fat: 15g
- Carbohydrates: 40g
- Fiber: 6g
- Sugar: 4g

Health Benefits:

- Tofu is a good source of plant-based protein and contains all nine essential amino acids.
- Vegetables provide essential vitamins, minerals, and antioxidants, contributing to overall health and well-being.
- This dish is low in saturated fat and cholesterol, making it heart-healthy and suitable for vegetarians.

## Packaging and Storing:

- Allow the stir-fried noodles with tofu and vegetables to cool slightly before storing.
- Store leftovers in an airtight container in the refrigerator for up to 3 days.
- Reheat in the microwave or on the stovetop until heated through before serving.

## Precautions:

- Press tofu properly to remove excess water and enhance its texture and flavor.
- Adjust the amount of soy sauce and sesame oil according to your taste preferences and dietary restrictions.
- Be mindful of the cooking time for noodles to avoid overcooking and becoming mushy.

## Safety Caution:

- Ensure tofu is cooked thoroughly to avoid any risk of foodborne illness.
- Use separate utensils and cutting boards for raw tofu and vegetables to prevent cross-contamination.
- Store leftovers promptly and refrigerate to prevent spoilage.

# Chapter 7

# Desert For Every Season

# Lemon Blueberry Cheesecake Bars

Ingredients:

For the Crust:

- 1 1/2 cups graham cracker crumbs
- 1/4 cup granulated sugar
- 1/2 cup unsalted butter, melted

For the Cheesecake Layer:

- 16 ounces cream cheese, softened
- 2/3 cup granulated sugar
- 2 large eggs
- 1 teaspoon vanilla extract
- Zest of 1 lemon

For the Blueberry Layer:

- 1 1/2 cups fresh blueberries
- 1/4 cup granulated sugar
- 1 tablespoon lemon juice
- 1 tablespoon cornstarch

Time of preparation:

- Preparation Time:20 minutes
- Baking: 35-40 minutes

- Cooling: 2 hours
- Total Time: Approximately 3 hours

Procedure:

- Preheat your oven to 350°F (175°C). To make removal easier, leave an overhanging piece of parchment paper on the sides of a 9 x 9-inch baking sheet.

Make the Crust:

- In a medium bowl, mix graham cracker crumbs, sugar, and melted butter until well combined.
- Evenly press the mixture into the bottom of the pan that has been prepared. For 8 to 10 minutes, bake until gently browned. Take it out of the oven and let it to cool a little.

Prepare the Cheesecake Layer:

- Beat the cream cheese and sugar together in a big bowl until creamy.
- One egg at a time, add them, and thoroughly mix each one in.
- Add the lemon zest and vanilla extract, stirring until well combined.
- Cover the chilled crust with the cheesecake mixture.

Make the Blueberry Layer:

- In a small saucepan, combine blueberries, sugar, lemon juice, and cornstarch.
- Cook over medium heat, stirring constantly until the mixture thickens and the blueberries burst, about 5-7 minutes.
- Remove from heat and let it cool slightly.
- Spoon the blueberry mixture over the cheesecake layer, spreading it evenly.

Bake the Bars:

- Bake for 25 to 30 minutes in a preheated oven, or until the center is still somewhat jiggly and the sides are set.
- Take it out of the oven and allow it to cool fully in the pan using a wire rack.
- Chill for a minimum of two hours prior to slicing into bars.

Tips and Tricks:

- Ensure the cream cheese is softened at room temperature to avoid lumps in the cheesecake layer.
- Use fresh blueberries for the best flavor and texture in the blueberry layer.
- Allow the cheesecake bars to cool completely before chilling in the refrigerator to prevent condensation on the surface.

Nutritional Value per Serving (1 bar):

- Calories: Approximately 280 kcal
- Fat: 18g
- Carbohydrates: 26g
- Protein: 4g

Health Benefits:

- Blueberries are rich in antioxidants and vitamins, promoting heart health and reducing the risk of chronic diseases.
- While cheesecake bars are indulgent treats, moderation is key to enjoying them within a balanced diet.

Packaging and Storing:Store

- lemon blueberry cheesecake bars in an airtight container in the refrigerator for up to 5 days.
- For longer storage, wrap individual bars tightly in plastic wrap and freeze for up to 2 months.
- Precautions and Post-Caution:
- Always handle hot pans and ingredients with care to prevent burns.
- Allow the cheesecake bars to cool completely before cutting to ensure clean slices.

Safety Caution:

- When baking, be cautious of hot surfaces and use oven mitts or towels to handle pans and trays.
- Ensure the oven is turned off after baking and avoid leaving hot appliances unattended.

# Chocolate Mint Avocado Mousse

Ingredients:

- 2 ripe avocados, peeled and pitted
- 1/4 cup cocoa powder
- 1/4 cup maple syrup or honey
- 1/4 cup coconut milk
- 1 teaspoon vanilla extract
- 1/2 teaspoon peppermint extract
- Pinch of salt
- Optional toppings: fresh mint leaves, chocolate shavings

Time of preparation :

- Preparation Time: 15 minutes
- Chilling: 1-2 hours
- Total Time: Approximately 1.5-2.5 hours

Procedure:

Blend the Ingredients:

- In a food processor or blender, combine the avocados, cocoa powder, maple syrup (or honey), coconut milk, vanilla extract, peppermint extract, and a pinch of salt.

- Blend until smooth and creamy, stopping occasionally to scrape down the edges to make sure everything is thoroughly mixed.

Chill the Mousse:

- Transfer the chocolate mint avocado mousse into serving bowls or glasses.
- Cover and refrigerate for at least 1-2 hours to allow the mousse to set and the flavors to meld.

Serve and Garnish:

- Before serving, garnish with fresh mint leaves and chocolate shavings if desired.
- Enjoy chilled!

Tips and Tricks:

- Use ripe avocados for a smoother texture and better flavor.
- Adjust the sweetness level by adding more or less maple syrup or honey according to your taste preferences.
- For a richer mousse, you can use full-fat coconut milk instead of light coconut milk.
- Make sure to blend the ingredients thoroughly to achieve a silky-smooth consistency.

Nutritional Value per Serving:

- Calories: Approximately 200 kcal
- Fat: 15g
- Carbohydrates: 17g
- Protein: 3g
- Fiber: 7g

Health Benefits:

- Avocados are loaded with healthy fats, fiber, and various nutrients, contributing to heart health and weight management.
- Cocoa powder is rich in antioxidants and may help improve heart health and reduce inflammation.
- This mousse is naturally sweetened with maple syrup or honey, making it a healthier alternative to traditional desserts.

Packaging and Storing:

- Store the chocolate mint avocado mousse in an airtight container in the refrigerator for up to 2 days.
- To prevent browning, press a piece of plastic wrap directly onto the surface of the mousse before refrigerating.

Precautions and Post-Caution:

- Make sure to use ripe avocados
- achieve the desired creamy texture.
- Keep the mousse chilled until ready to serve to maintain its freshness and consistency.

Safety Caution:

- When using kitchen appliances such as blenders or food processors, follow the manufacturer's instructions and handle them with care to avoid accidents.
- Always check the avocados for ripeness and discard any spoiled or rotten parts before using them in the recipe.

# Seasonal Fruit Sorbet

Ingredients:

- 4 cups seasonal fruits (such as berries, mangoes, peaches, or melons), washed, peeled, and chopped
- 1/2 cup granulated sugar (adjust according to the sweetness of the fruits)
- 1/4 cup water
- One tablespoon of optional lemon juice (for extra freshness)

Time of preparation:

- Preparation Time: 15 minutes
- Freezing: 4-6 hours
- Total Time: Approximately 4.5-6.5 hours

Procedure:

Prepare the Fruit:

- Wash, peel (if necessary), and chop the seasonal fruits into small pieces.

Make the Simple Syrup:

- Add the water and the granulated sugar to a small saucepan.
- Stir continuously while heating over medium heat until all of the sugar melts.
- After taking off the heat, allow the simple syrup to reach room temperature.

Blend the Ingredients:

- In a blender or food processor, combine the chopped fruits, cooled simple syrup, and lemon juice (if using).
- Blend until smooth and well combined.

Chill the Mixture:

- Transfer the fruit mixture to a shallow, freezer-safe container or baking dish.
- Put a lid on it or cover it with plastic wrap, then freeze.

Freeze the Sorbet:

- Every 30 minutes, remove the sorbet from the freezer and stir vigorously with a fork to break up any ice crystals.
- For the first two to three hours, repeat this technique every thirty minutes..

Serve the Sorbet:

- Once the sorbet reaches the desired consistency (smooth and scoopable), serve immediately in chilled bowls or glasses.

Tips and Tricks:

- Use ripe and flavorful seasonal fruits for the best-tasting sorbet.
- Adjust the amount of sugar according to the sweetness of the fruits and your personal preference.
- Adding lemon juice helps enhance the flavors of the fruits and prevents them from oxidizing.
- For a smoother texture, strain the fruit mixture through a fine-mesh sieve before freezing.

Nutritional Value per Serving:

- Calories: Approximately 100 kcal
- Fat: 0g
- Carbohydrates: 25g
- Fiber: 3g
- Protein: 1g

Health Benefits:

- Seasonal fruits are rich in vitamins, minerals, and antioxidants, which support overall health and immunity.
- Sorbets are a healthier alternative to ice cream, as they contain less fat and calories while still offering a refreshing treat.

Packaging and Storing:

- Store the seasonal fruit sorbet in an airtight container in the freezer for up to 1 month.
- To prevent freezer burn, cover the sorbet with a layer of plastic wrap before sealing the container.

Precautions and Post-Caution:

- Make sure to stir the sorbet mixture regularly during the freezing process to prevent it from becoming too icy.
- Avoid over-freezing the sorbet, as it may become too hard to scoop.

Safety Caution:

- When handling sharp objects such as knives or blenders, exercise caution to prevent accidents.
- Store sorbet containers securely in the freezer to avoid spills or leaks.

# Chapter 8

# Tips And Trick

# Guide to Seasonal Produce for Seasonal Cooking

Seasonal cooking is not only a culinary practice but also a way to connect with nature's rhythms and enjoy the freshest, most flavorful ingredients available during each time of the year. Understanding what fruits and vegetables are in season can greatly enhance your cooking experience, allowing you to create dishes that are not only delicious but also more sustainable and economical. Here's a comprehensive guide to seasonal produce for seasonal cooking:

Spring

Fruits:

- Strawberries
- Rhubarb
- Apricots
- Cherries
- Pineapple
- Mangoes

Vegetables:

- Asparagus
- Artichokes
- Peas
- Spinach
- Lettuce
- Radishes
- Arugula
- Fennel
- Spring onions
- Broccoli
- Cauliflower

Summer

Fruits:

- Berries (blueberries, raspberries, blackberries)
- Watermelon
- Cantaloupe
- Peaches
- Plums
- Nectarines
- Tomatoes
- Kiwi
- Grapes
- Lemons
- Limes

Vegetables:

- Corn
- Zucchini
- Eggplant
- Bell peppers
- Cucumbers
- Green beans
- Summer squash
- Okra
- Beets
- Carrots
- Radishes
- Swiss chard

Fall

Fruits:

- Apples
- Pears
- Grapes
- Persimmons
- Cranberries
- Pomegranates

- Figs

Vegetables:

- Pumpkins
- Squash (butternut, acorn, spaghetti)
- Sweet potatoes
- Brussels sprouts
- Cauliflower
- Broccoli
- Cabbage
- Kale
- Turnips
- Rutabagas
- Mushrooms

Winter

Fruits:

- Citrus fruits (oranges, grapefruits, mandarins)
- Kiwi
- Pomegranates
- Persimmons
- Apples

Vegetables:

- Brussels sprouts
- Cauliflower
- Cabbage
- Kale
- Carrots
- Parsnips
- Turnips
- Rutabagas
- Potatoes
- Winter squash (butternut, acorn, spaghetti)

# Tips for Seasonal Cooking:

Visit Farmers' Markets: Local farmers' markets are excellent places to find fresh, seasonal produce. Chatting with farmers can give you insights into what's in season and how to best utilize the ingredients.

Plan Your Meals Around Seasonal Ingredients:

Embrace the ingredients that are in season and plan your meals accordingly. This not only ensures freshness but also supports local agriculture.

Experiment with Preservation Techniques:

To enjoy seasonal flavors year-round, experiment with preservation techniques such as canning, freezing, and pickling. This allows you to enjoy your favorite seasonal produce even when it's out of season.

Be Creative:

Seasonal cooking encourages creativity in the kitchen. Experiment with different flavor combinations and cooking methods to make the most of seasonal ingredients.

Consider the Environment:

Choosing seasonal produce often means selecting fruits and vegetables that are locally grown, reducing the carbon footprint associated with transportation and storage.
By following this guide to seasonal produce, you can embark on a culinary journey that celebrates the best flavors each season has to offer. Whether you're whipping up light spring salads, refreshing summer smoothies, hearty fall stews, or comforting winter soups, seasonal cooking allows you to savor the essence of each season in every bite.

Stocking a Seasonal Pantry for Seasonal Cooking

Stocking a seasonal pantry is a crucial aspect of seasonal cooking, ensuring you have the necessary ingredients on hand to create delicious and nutritious meals that celebrate the flavors of each season. A well-stocked pantry enables you to prepare meals efficiently and make the most of fresh, seasonal produce. Here's a detailed guide to stocking your pantry for seasonal cooking:

Assessing Your Pantry:

Before stocking your pantry, take inventory of what you already have. Discard expired items and organize your pantry space to make room for new additions. Consider the staples you use regularly and those you'll need to accommodate seasonal cooking.

Staple Ingredients for Every Season:

Regardless of the season, certain pantry staples are essential for versatile cooking. These include:

- Grains: Rice, quinoa, pasta, couscous, oats
- Legumes: Lentils, beans (black beans, chickpeas, kidney beans)
- Canned Goods: Tomatoes, coconut milk, broth (vegetable, chicken, or beef), beans
- Oils and Vinegars: Olive oil, vegetable oil, balsamic vinegar, red wine vinegar, apple cider vinegar
- Herbs and Spices: Salt, black pepper, garlic powder, onion powder, paprika, cumin, cinnamon, dried herbs (oregano, thyme, rosemary, basil)

- Condiments: Soy sauce, Worcestershire sauce, mustard, honey, maple syrup

Seasonal Additions to Your Pantry:

- In addition to staple ingredients, incorporate seasonal items into your pantry to align with the flavors of each season:

Spring:

- Preserved Lemons: Brighten up dishes with the zesty flavor of preserved lemons, perfect for adding a burst of freshness to salads, marinades, and sauces.
- Artichoke Hearts: Canned or jarred artichoke hearts add depth and richness to springtime pasta dishes, salads, and dips.
- Green Lentils: Nutrient-rich green lentils are versatile and can be used in soups, salads, and vegetarian mains.

Summer:

- Pesto: Stock up on basil pesto to toss with freshly harvested tomatoes, pasta, or spread on sandwiches and pizzas for a taste of summer.
- Pickles: Homemade or store-bought pickles are a refreshing addition to summer sandwiches, salads, and charcuterie boards.
- Salsa: Keep jars of salsa on hand for quick and easy summer dips, toppings for grilled meats and seafood, or flavoring for tacos and quesadillas.

Fall:

- Canned Pumpkin: Embrace the flavors of fall with canned pumpkin puree, perfect for making soups, stews, baked goods, and creamy pasta sauces.
- Apple Butter: Spread apple butter on toast, biscuits, or use it as a sweetener in fall-inspired desserts and glazes for roasted meats.
- Cranberry Sauce: Use cranberry sauce as a condiment for roasted poultry, stir it into oatmeal or yogurt, or swirl it into muffin and cake batters for a burst of tartness.

Winter:

- Chestnuts: Incorporate roasted chestnuts into savory dishes like soups, stuffing, and risottos, or use them in desserts such as cakes and tarts.

- Dried Fruit: Stock up on dried fruits like figs, dates, and apricots to add sweetness and texture to winter salads, grain dishes, and baked goods.
- Canned Soups: Keep a variety of canned soups on hand for quick and comforting meals on chilly winter nights.

# Tips for Organizing Your Seasonal Pantry:

- Label and Date Items: Proper labeling and dating help you keep track of the freshness of your pantry items and prevent waste.
- Rotate Stock: Regularly rotate your pantry items to ensure that older items are used before newer ones.
- Keep Essentials Visible: Put products that are used regularly at eye level and items that are used less frequently higher or lower on the shelf.Invest in Storage Containers: Invest in airtight storage containers to keep pantry items fresh and organized.
- Plan Ahead: Plan your meals based on seasonal ingredients and make a shopping list to restock your pantry as needed.
- By stocking your pantry with seasonal ingredients and staples, you'll be well-equipped to create delicious meals year-round that highlight the best flavors each season has to offer. Whether you're cooking light and fresh spring salads, indulging in summer grilling, savoring hearty fall stews, or cozying up with comforting winter soups, a well-stocked seasonal pantry is the foundation of flavorful and nourishing seasonal cooking.

# Substituting Ingredients Based on Season

Substituting ingredients based on the season is a valuable skill in seasonal cooking, allowing you to adapt recipes to make the most of what's fresh and available during different times of the year. Whether a particular fruit, vegetable, or spice is out of season or not readily available, knowing how to substitute ingredients can ensure your dishes remain flavorful and satisfying. Here's a detailed guide on substituting ingredients based on the season:

Understanding Seasonal Ingredient Substitution:

Seasonal ingredient substitution involves replacing certain items in recipes with alternatives that are in season or more readily available during a specific time of the year. This not only allows you to maintain the integrity of the dish but also ensures that you're using fresh, flavorful ingredients.

Spring Substitutions:

- Asparagus: Substitute with green beans or snap peas.
- Artichokes: Replace with green beans or snap peas.
- Spinach: Use Swiss chard or kale as alternatives.
- Rhubarb: Try substituting with cranberries or tart apples.
- Strawberries: Replace with raspberries, blackberries, or blueberries.

Summer Substitutions:

- Tomatoes: During winter, use canned tomatoes or sun-dried tomatoes for a more concentrated flavor.
- Zucchini: Substitute with yellow squash, eggplant, or cucumbers.
- Corn: Use frozen corn kernels when fresh corn is out of season.
- Berries: Experiment with frozen berries or stone fruits such as peaches or plums.
- Herbs: Grow your own indoor herbs or use dried herbs if fresh ones are not available

Fall Substitutions:

- Pumpkin: Swap with butternut squash or sweet potatoes.
- Apples: Try using pears or quinces in place of apples.
- Brussels Sprouts: Substitute with cabbage or broccoli.
- Cranberries: Use pomegranate seeds or dried cherries as alternatives.
- Pears: Replace with apples or persimmons in recipes.

Winter Substitutions:

- Citrus Fruits: Use lemon or lime juice as substitutes for oranges or grapefruits.
- Root Vegetables: Experiment with different varieties of root vegetables such as parsnips, turnips, or rutabagas.
- Winter Squash: Swap butternut squash with acorn squash or pumpkin.
- Dark Leafy Greens: Substitute spinach with Swiss chard or kale.
- Nuts: Replace walnuts or almonds with pecans or hazelnuts in recipes.

# Tips for Successful Ingredient Substitution:

- Consider Flavor Profiles: Choose substitutes that complement the flavors of the original ingredient and maintain the overall taste of the dish.
- Be Mindful of Textures: Pay attention to the texture of the substitute ingredient to ensure it works well in the recipe.
- Adjust Cooking Times: Some substitutions may require adjustments to cooking times and methods to achieve the desired results.
- Experiment and Adapt: Don't be afraid to experiment with ingredient substitutions and adapt recipes based on what's available and in season.
- Stay Flexible: Embrace the flexibility of seasonal cooking and be open to trying new flavor combinations and ingredient substitutions.
- By understanding how to substitute ingredients based on the season, you can adapt recipes to reflect the flavors of each season and make the most of what's available locally and seasonally. Whether you're cooking light and fresh spring dishes, embracing the abundance of summer produce, enjoying the hearty flavors of fall, or

savoring comforting winter meals, ingredient substitution allows you to create delicious and satisfying dishes year-round.

- Seasonal cooking offers a culinary journey that celebrates the ever-changing flavors and bounties of nature throughout the year. As we conclude our exploration of seasonal cooking, it becomes evident that this approach to culinary artistry is more than just a trend; it's a philosophy that fosters a deeper connection to the natural world, encourages sustainability, and inspires creativity in the kitchen.
- Through our guide to seasonal produce, stocking a seasonal pantry, and substituting ingredients based on the season, we've uncovered the richness and versatility of seasonal cooking. By embracing ingredients at their peak freshness, we not only enjoy superior flavors and nutritional benefits but also support local farmers and reduce our environmental footprint.
- Seasonal cooking invites us to be mindful and resourceful, encouraging us to adapt recipes based on what's available and in season. It challenges us to experiment with new flavors, textures, and cooking techniques, fostering a sense of culinary exploration and discovery.
- Moreover, seasonal cooking is a celebration of tradition and culture, reflecting the diverse culinary heritage of regions around the world. It allows us to connect with our roots, honor seasonal festivals and rituals, and share meaningful meals with family and friends.
- In conclusion, seasonal cooking is a holistic approach to gastronomy that nourishes both body and soul. It encourages us to savor the essence of each season, appreciate the beauty of nature's cycles, and delight in the simple pleasures of food shared with loved ones. As we embark on our culinary journey through the seasons, let us embrace the flavors, aromas, and memories that make each meal a celebration of life's abundance.

# conclusion

Seasonal cooking offers a culinary journey that celebrates the ever-changing flavors and bounties of nature throughout the year. As we conclude our exploration of seasonal cooking, it becomes evident that this approach to culinary artistry is more than just a trend;

it's a philosophy that fosters a deeper connection to the natural world, encourages sustainability, and inspires creativity in the kitchen.

Through our guide to seasonal produce, stocking a seasonal pantry, and substituting ingredients based on the season, we've uncovered the richness and versatility of seasonal cooking. By embracing ingredients at their peak freshness, we not only enjoy superior flavors and nutritional benefits but also support local farmers and reduce our environmental footprint.

Seasonal cooking invites us to be mindful and resourceful, encouraging us to adapt recipes based on what's available and in season. It challenges us to experiment with new flavors, textures, and cooking techniques, fostering a sense of culinary exploration and discovery.

Moreover, seasonal cooking is a celebration of tradition and culture, reflecting the diverse culinary heritage of regions around the world. It allows us to connect with our roots, honor seasonal festivals and rituals, and share meaningful meals with family and friends.Sseasonal cooking is a holistic approach to gastronomy that nourishes both body and soul. It encourages us to savor the essence of each season, appreciate the beauty of nature's cycles, and delight in the simple pleasures of food shared with loved ones. As we embark on our culinary journey through the seasons, let us embrace the flavors, aromas, and memories that make each meal a celebration of life's abundance.